Swedish Americans

TIFFANY PETERSON

Heinemann Library
Chicago, Illinois

Designed by Roslyn Broder
Photo research by Julie Laffin
Printed in China by WKT Company Limited

08 07 06 05 04
10 9 8 7 6 5 4 3 2 1

Library of Congress Cataloging-in-Publication Data
Peterson, Tiffany.
  Swedish Americans / Tiffany Peterson.
     p. cm. -- (We are America)
  Summary: An overview of the history and daily lives of Swedish people who immigrated to the United States.
  Includes bibliographical references (p.) and index.
  ISBN 1-4034-5024-2
  1. Swedish Americans--History--Juvenile literature. 2. Swedish Americans--Social life and customs--Juvenile literature. [1. Swedish Americans.] I. Title. II. Series.
  E184.S23P46 2004
  973'.04397--dc22
                              2003021704

Acknowledgments
The author and publisher are grateful to the following for permission to reproduce copyright material:
pp. 4, 5, 28, 29 Courtesy of Sandi Ekstam; p. 7 John Corbett/Ecoscene/Corbis; p. 8 Alamy Images; p. 9 Joseph Sohm/Corbis; pp. 10, 15 Corbis; pp. 11, 12 Brown Brothers; p. 14 Minnesota Historical Society/Corbis; p. 16 Fred Hulstrand History In Pictures Collection/NDIRS-NDSU, Fargo/Library of Congress; p. 17 The Granger Collection, New York; p. 18 Courtesy of Hal Bern; p. 19 Chicago Historical Society; pp. 20, 22 Beryl Goldberg Photographer; pp. 21, 26 Greg Ryan/Sally Beyer; p. 23 Ted Spiegel/Corbis; pp. 24, 25 Michael John Kelly; p. 27 Reed Saxon/AP Wide World Photos

Cover photographs by Minnesota Historical Society

The author wishes to thank Sandi Ekstam, Becky Ekstam, Hal Bern, and Brian Krumm for their help. Special thanks to Sara Ranne, a Swedish-American translator and volunteer at the Swedish American Museum Center in Chicago, for her comments in preparation of this book.

Some quotations and material used in this book come from the following sources. In some cases, quotes have been abridged or edited for clarity: p. 9 *America Fever: A Swede in the West: 1914–1923* by Erick H. Youngquist (Nashville, Tenn.: Voyageur Publishing Co., 1990); p. 11 *Ellis Island Interviews: In Their Own Words* by Peter Morton Coan (New York: Facts on File, 1998); p. 12 *American Immigration* by Grolier Educational Staff (Danbury, Conn.: Scholastic Library, 1998).

Every effort has been made to contact copyright holders of any material reproduced in this book. Any omissions will be rectified in subsequent printings if notice is given to the publisher.

On the cover of this book, Swedish immigrant Halsten Bollman and his family are shown in about 1880. A photograph of Swede Hollow, an area in St. Paul, Minnesota, where many Swedish immigrants settled in the late 1850s, is shown in the background.

Contents

Some words are shown in bold, **like this.** You can find out what they mean by looking in the glossary.

A New Home

Like many other Swedish-American immigrants, Märta moved to Chicago, Illinois.

In 1903, Märta Källström was born in Jämtland, an area in western Sweden. She had fun growing up in Sweden. She liked to hike in the mountains and pick berries. However, many Swedish people were unhappy. In the late 1800s, thousands of them moved to the United States. There were not enough jobs in Sweden, and food was **scarce.** Some of Märta's brothers and sisters had already moved to the United States and lived in Chicago, Illinois.

After she went to the United States, Märta started using a name that sounded more American. Her new name was Martha Challstrom.

When Märta was 24 years old, she decided to **immigrate** to the United States, too. In 1927, she left Sweden. A few weeks later, she arrived at the Ellis Island Immigration Station in New York City. Doctors there gave her a checkup and said she was sick. So, she had to stay at Ellis Island for several weeks. Finally, when the doctors said she was healthy, she left and traveled to Chicago. She started working as a maid. She had to work hard to support herself.

I always think she must have been a bit of a tomboy and very courageous to come to America and work on her own. She worked hard at a time when women generally didn't venture outside the home.

—Sandi Ekstam, speaking about her mother,

Martha Challstrom

Sweden

Sweden is a country in northern Europe. The country is about the same size as the state of California. Sweden is a beautiful country. There are many mountains, plains, forests, rivers, and lakes. Most people live in the south of Sweden, where the land is mostly flat. Sweden is located between Norway and Finland. These countries, along with Denmark, are known as the Scandinavian countries.

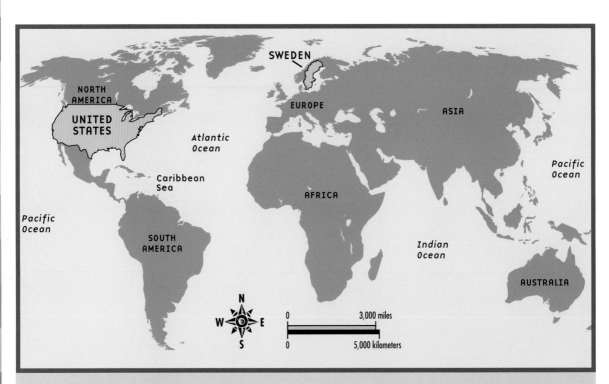

This map shows where Sweden and the United States are located in the world. About nine million people live in Sweden.

*Forests cover more than half of the land in Sweden.
This photo shows cabins next to a lake in Sweden.*

In the late 1800s, the number of people living in Sweden was increasing. People knew how to take better care of themselves, so they lived longer. Also, there had been a long period of peacetime for Sweden. Soldiers had not been sent to deadly wars. As the population grew, there was no longer enough land for everyone to farm. Many Swedish people started thinking about moving away from Sweden to where land was available.

The northern area of Sweden is called the Land of the Midnight Sun. For about eight weeks during the summer, the sun shines 24 hours a day there.

Early Swedish Immigrants

In 1638, the first group of Swedish people, also called Swedes, came to North America. They formed a **colony** named New Sweden near what is today the city of Wilmington, Delaware. The colonists took furs and other items from the colony back to Sweden to sell. Dutch **immigrants** took over the colony in 1655. The Swedish government did not fight to keep the colony because the Swedish colonists were not making enough money there. Traveling to Sweden and back to sell goods was too expensive.

This is what the Old Swedes Church in Wilmington, Delaware, looks like today. Swedish immigrants helped build the church. It was completed in 1699.

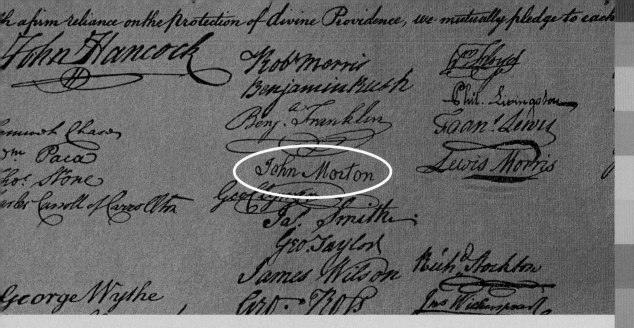

*The **Declaration of Independence** shows the signature of John Morton, an early Swedish American.*

It was not until the 1860s that large numbers of Swedes began immigrating to the United States. They had several reasons for leaving Sweden. Besides a lack of farmland, Swedes had suffered through several years of bad weather. Farmers' crops had been destroyed by **droughts** and flooding. Many Swedes did not have enough to eat. People began to immigrate to the United States, hoping to live better lives.

Most of us were **seasick**, and when I was on **deck**, I spent a good deal of time at the railing. Late one evening, after eleven days at sea, we finally sighted land. You can imagine how thrilled I was.

—Erick Youngquist, who immigrated from Sweden when he was twenty years old

The Journey

In the mid-1800s, **immigrants** often left Sweden as a group. Families would travel together after selling their farms and packing whatever they could take with them. They usually started their journey by taking a train to Göteborg, Sweden. There, they would board a **cargo** ship. The cost was low, but the journey was difficult. These ships were built to carry goods, not passengers. Passengers often had to bring enough food with them to last for the trip.

This photo shows a ship that Swedish immigrants might have traveled to the United States on in the early 1900s.

This photo shows immigrants from Scandinavia arriving in the United States.

Beginning in the 1860s, immigrants could travel on passenger ships. The conditions were better, and the journey was shorter—usually ten to fourteen days. However, many immigrants could only afford tickets for **steerage** class. In the late 1800s and early 1900s, it was common for one family member to go to the United States alone. The rest of the family would wait for a letter that included tickets for others to go to the United States.

> Before I left Sweden, I had to go to a doctor and get a clean bill of health . . . that I had been **vaccinated.**
> I remember on the ship they examined my head for lice.
> —Caren Lundgren, who immigrated in 1921 at age 18

Arriving in the United States

Ships bringing **immigrants** to the United States usually landed off the coast of New York. The early Swedish immigrants spent their first hours in the United States at an immigration station in New York City. There, **officials** questioned them. They had to give their names and tell where they were born. They told the officials if they planned to stay in New York or go somewhere else.

I landed on Ellis Island in August 1921. Of course, hundreds of immigrants were there, all talking different languages.

—Sonya Anna Thornblom who immigrated from Sweden when she was 12 years old

*These two Swedish children came to the United States wearing **traditional** Swedish clothing. They arrived in New York.*

After 1850, many Swedish immigrants traveled by train from Chicago to other cities in the U.S. This map shows some cities and states that Swedish people first moved to and where many Swedish Americans still live today.

Most Swedish immigrants left New York and continued on to the Midwest. Immigrants who arrived in and before the 1850s boarded another boat. This boat took them down the Hudson River, to the Erie **Canal**, and across the Great Lakes to Chicago. Many Swedish immigrants stayed in Chicago. Later immigrants traveled from Chicago by train or by horse into Minnesota, Iowa, Kansas, Nebraska, and other cities in Illinois, such as Rock Island and Rockford.

"America Fever"

By 1880, most people in Sweden knew at least one person who had moved to the United States. Some Swedes who became successful traveled back to Sweden for visits. They described the great opportunities in the United States. Other Swedish Americans wrote letters to family members and friends in Sweden. Local newspapers would often print the letters so the whole town could read about the person's travels and success. The success stories had a big effect on people in Sweden.

The population of the town of Millesvik in Sweden was cut in half between 1865 and 1910 because of immigration. During the 1880s, one out of every seven Swedes immigrated.

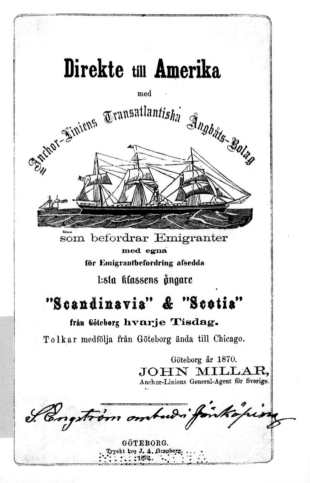

This is a page from an 1870 Swedish book written about immigrants going to the U.S.

Time Line

1638	Swedish **immigrants** start the New Sweden **colony.**
1800–1900	The population of Sweden grows from 2.3 million to 5.1 million people.
1845–1854	About 15,000 Swedes immigrate to the United States to find land or jobs.
1868–1880	More than 100,000 Swedes escape **famine** and poor conditions by immigrating to the U.S.
1881–1890	"America Fever" hits Sweden and about 450,000 people leave Sweden.
1891–1930	Letters from the U.S. help about 700,000 Swedes decide to immigrate to the U.S.

Partly as a result of the immigrants' success stories, "America Fever" swept across Sweden. Many people wanted to find a way to get to America. About 450,000 Swedes chose to leave their homeland and move to the United States in the 1880s. They went to look for land, jobs, freedom, and new ways of living.

This photo shows a Swedish American reading a Swedish newspaper in 1942 in Minnesota.

Land and Lumber

Most early Swedish **immigrants** had been farmers before they came to the United States. Many of them had immigrated in order to have farmland of their own. The **Homestead** Act of 1862 said that anyone in the United States who was at least 21 years old could have 160 acres of land for free. The person had to live on the land, build a house on it, and farm on it for five years.

Homesteading was hard work. Homesteaders moved into new areas of the United States where there had been nothing but forests and prairies. They cleared the land and built houses.

This gathering at a farm in North Dakota probably included some Swedish Americans. The photo was taken in about 1897.

16

This Swedish immigrant arrived in New York City in about 1905. Many Swedish immigrants stayed in cities in the U.S. to find work.

Swedish immigrants traveled to the Midwest, the Great Plains, and the West to claim land. Kansas, Nebraska, Minnesota, and Illinois all attracted large numbers of Swedes. Swedish immigrants also moved into Washington, Oregon, and California. There, many worked on railroads or for lumber companies. Some of them worked as lumberjacks. Others worked at sawmills, where they cut trees into wood for building houses or furniture.

Swedish immigrants introduced log cabins to the United States. When they cut down trees to clear an area for farming, they saved the tree trunks. The trunks became the walls of their homes.

17

Life in the Cities

While many Swedish **immigrants** became farmers, many others remained in cities. In the early 1900s, Chicago had the second-largest Swedish population of all cities in the world. It was second only to Stockholm, the capital and largest city in Sweden. In the cities, Swedish immigrants worked at many different types of jobs. Many men worked in factories. Women were often maids or did sewing work.

Between 1890 and 1930, Swedish was the most common language in Andersonville, a neighborhood in Chicago.

Like many Swedish immigrants, Severin Winberg and Anna Sofia Jonsdottir met in the United States. They were later married and lived in Galesburg, Illinois.

These are the types of houses that some Swedish Americans lived in. The photo was taken in an area of Chicago with a large Swedish-American population in about 1880.

While Swedish Americans living in cities did not have the hardships of clearing land to farm, they had their own difficulties. Many had trouble finding jobs because they did not speak English well. Also, many Swedish Americans had only enough money to live in crowded, rundown neighborhoods. The dirty conditions caused by overcrowding made diseases spread quickly.

After the Great Chicago Fire destroyed much of the city in 1871, Swedish Americans helped rebuild. In fact, their involvement led to the saying "Swedes built Chicago."

Swedish-American Culture

Most Swedish **immigrants** wanted to become American citizens as soon as possible. Many even changed their names to sound more American. For example, someone with the last name Svenson might have changed it to Swanson. This did not mean that they gave up Swedish **culture** and **traditions,** however. In fact, many Swedish-American organizations were started to preserve these things. Many of the organizations are still operating today.

My mom spoke Swedish to my dad and my aunts and uncles when she didn't want me to know what was going on—I used to be able to understand a bit of it. They both learned English well and never wanted me or my sister to speak Swedish.
—Sandi Ekstam, daughter of Swedish immigrants Martha and Andrew Ostlund

These people attended a Swedish Midsummer festival in New York City's Central Park.

These dancers performed in Minneapolis, Minnesota, as part of a Swedish celebration called Svenskarnas Dag, *or Swedish Day.*

One of these organizations is the Vasa Order of America. It is named after Gustav Vasa, the king of Sweden from 1523–1560. The Vasa Order was created more than 100 years ago to help Swedish immigrants. Today, more than 300 Vasa lodges in the United States, Canada, and Sweden hold events to celebrate Swedish holidays, such as **Saint** Lucia Day. Museums such as the Swedish American Museum Center in Chicago have also opened to educate people about Swedish Americans.

Gustav Vasa had to leave Sweden to escape Denmark's invading army. However, two Swedish skiers raced 56 miles (90 kilometers) to catch up with him. Swedes who wanted Vasa's help in freeing Sweden from Danish rule sent the skiers. This event is celebrated every year in Sweden with a ski race called the *Vasaloppet*.

Celebrations

Swedish people celebrate the summer **solstice,** which is the longest day of the year, in late June. On this day in Sweden, some sunlight is visible even in the middle of the night. The celebration, called Midsummer, lasts an entire weekend and includes food, games, and music. Swedish Americans also celebrate Midsummer. They dress in **traditional** Swedish clothes, eat Swedish food, and listen to Swedish music.

The raising of the **maypole** *is a common event at Midsummer celebrations. Children often decorate the maypole with flowers and leaves.*

These girls held candles and sang on Saint Lucia Day in the Old Swedes' Church in Philadelphia, Pennsylvania.

Many Swedish Americans also celebrate **Saint** Lucia Day on December 13. It is the start of Swedish Christmas celebrations. In Sweden, many towns choose a girl from the town to dress up as Saint Lucia. The girl wears a long, white gown and a crown of candles. She leads a parade of girls carrying candles through the town. Some Swedish-American families have their own Saint Lucia Day celebration. One daughter is chosen to be "Lucia." She serves coffee and treats such as sweet rolls to family members in the morning.

Swedish Food and Dining

Swedish Americans introduced new foods and ways of dining to the United States. A smorgasbord is a way of serving food that Swedes brought to the U.S. Many different types of food are set out on a long table. Included in the smorgasbord might be lunch meat, fish, boiled potatoes, and pickled beets. Other **traditional** Swedish foods, such as Swedish meatballs, are also served.

The word *smorgasbord* comes from the Swedish words that mean "open sandwich" and "table."

This photo shows the Swedish Bakery in Chicago. Since about 1928, the bakery has offered people in Chicago traditional Swedish baked goods.

24

This gourmet food store in Chicago has a variety of foods from Sweden for sale. They also sell homemade Swedish meatballs, seen at the bottom of the photo.

Swedish pancakes are popular as a breakfast dish in the United States. In Sweden, however, pancakes are usually served with ice cream or whipped cream for dessert after dinner. They are much thinner than the pancakes most Americans are used to eating. Breakfast in Sweden is usually thought of as the most important meal of the day. *Müsli,* a type of cereal, and sandwiches are served.

Arts and Entertainment

Like all Americans, Swedish Americans enjoy being entertained. There are a large number of Swedish Americans who work as entertainers. As early as 1850, Americans were introduced to Swedish musical talent. That year, a Swedish singer named Jenny Lind performed in hundreds of cities in the United States. She moved back to Sweden after two and a half years, but she gave thousands of dollars to help Swedish Americans.

Karen Branzell and Jussi Bjoerling are two famous Swedish-American singers. Both performed with the New York Metropolitan Opera.

These girls performed Swedish vocal music at a Swedish Day celebration in Minnesota.

Candice Bergen, a Swedish-American actor, won four Emmy Awards for her work on the television show Murphy Brown.

There are also many Swedish-American actors. Candice Bergen, whose father was from Sweden, is famous for her roles on the TV show *Murphy Brown* and in many films. Another famous Swedish-American actor was Greta Garbo. She was born in Sweden and **immigrated** to the United States in the 1920s. She became popular after appearing in films in the 1920s and 1930s.

A Swedish-American Family

In 1928, Martha Challstrom met Andrew Ostlund in Chicago. He was also Swedish. The two were later married and had two daughters, Marta and Sandi. Life in Chicago in the 1930s was difficult and dangerous. Many Americans were poor and did not have jobs. Chicago was also home to Al Capone and other **gangsters.** Andrew was nearly shot while he was driving one night. Martha and Andrew decided to move to Minnesota, where it would be safer for their family.

Martha enjoyed sewing, cooking, and gardening. She died in 1958.

In this photo, Martha and Andrew pose with their daughter, Marta, in Chicago.

The Ostlund family moved to Slayton, Minnesota, in 1946. Martha's sister and her sister's husband had a large farm there. Andrew opened a hardware store. He was a generous man, and he allowed his customers to buy things on **credit.** Much of the money was never paid, and he lost the store. So he went to work for the United States Air Force. Like many other Swedish Americans, the Ostlunds had some hard times. But they always stuck together as a family and worked hard to realize their dreams.

This photo shows Sandi Ekstam, Martha and Andrew's daughter, in 1953. She was five years old.

I think for kids to understand and be proud of what their **immigrant ancestors** did so that they could be born in America is really important.

—Sandi Ekstam

Swedish Immigration Chart

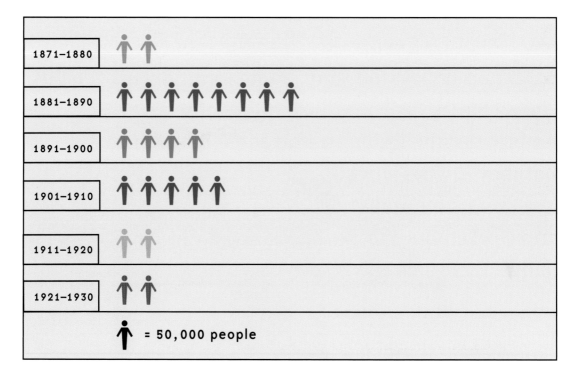

1871–1880	♀ ♀
1881–1890	♀ ♀ ♀ ♀ ♀ ♀ ♀ ♀
1891–1900	♀ ♀ ♀ ♀
1901–1910	♀ ♀ ♀ ♀ ♀
1911–1920	♀ ♀
1921–1930	♀ ♀

♀ = 50,000 people

*The largest number of Swedish **immigrants** came to the United States in the late 1800s.*

Source: U.S. Immigration and Naturalization Service

More Books to Read

Gunderson, Cory Gideon. *Swedish Americans.* Philadelphia, Pa.: Chelsea House Publishers, 2003.

Olson, Kay Melchisedech. *Norwegian, Swedish, and Danish Immigrants, 1820-1920.* Mankato, Minn.: Blue Earth Books, 2002.

Raatma, Lucia. *Swedish Americans.* Chanhassen, Minn.: Child's World, 2003.

Glossary

ancestor person who you are related to and who was born before you, like your mother, father, or grandparent

canal ditch dug and filled with water so that boats can cross a stretch of land. Canals are also used to get water to crops.

cargo goods that are shipped from one place to another. A cargo ship usually does not have rooms for passengers.

colony territory that is owned or ruled by another country

credit method of buying something and promising to pay for it later

culture ideas, skills, arts, and way of life for a certain group of people

Declaration of Independence document that in 1776 said that the American colonies were no longer under the control of Great Britain

drought long period of time with little or no rain

famine period of time when people do not have enough to eat

gangster member of a gang of criminals

homestead to live and build on a piece of land that was given for that purpose. People who homestead are called homesteaders.

immigrate to come to a country to live there for a long time. A person who immigrates in an immigrant.

maypole tall pole that is decorated with flowers and ribbons as part of a summer celebration

official officer whose job is to make sure people follow rules or directions

saint holy person

scarce not plentiful or difficult to find

seasick sick in the stomach due to a ship's rocking motion

solstice time of year when the sun is furthest north. The summer solstice is the longest day of the year.

steerage place on a ship where passengers who pay the least to travel stay

tradition belief or practice handed down through the years from one generation to the next

vaccinate to inject weak germs in a person to protect against a disease

Index